Life During the
AMERICAN REVOLUTION

By Kristen Rajczak

Gareth Stevens
Publishing

Please visit our website, www.garethstevens.com. For a free color catalog of all our high-quality books, call toll free 1-800-542-2595 or fax 1-877-542-2596.

Library of Congress Cataloging-in-Publication Data

Rajczak, Kristen.
 Life during the American Revolution / Kristen Rajczak.
   p. cm. – (What you didn't know about history)
 Includes index.
ISBN 978-1-4339-8425-9 (pbk.)
ISBN 978-1-4339-8426-6 (6-pack)
ISBN 978-1-4339-8424-2 (library binding)
1. United States–History—Revolution, 1775-1783—Social aspects. 2. United States—Social life and customs—1775-1783. 3. United States—Social conditions—To 1865. I. Title.
E163.R35 2013
973.3—dc23

                                   2012019735

First Edition

Published in 2013 by
Gareth Stevens Publishing
111 East 14th Street, Suite 349
New York, NY 10003

Copyright © 2013 Gareth Stevens Publishing

Designer: Daniel Hosek and Michael Flynn
Editor: Kristen Rajczak

Photo credits: Cover, pp. 1, 15 SuperStock/Getty Images; p. 5 Hulton Archive/Getty Images; p. 7 Interim Archives/Archive Photos/Getty Images; p. 9 Fotosearch/Archive Photos/Getty Images; p. 11 3LH-Fine Art/SuperStock/Getty Images; p. 13 Stock Montage/Archive Photos/ Getty Images; p. 17 Kean Collection/Archive Photos/Getty Images; p. 19 courtesy of Library of Congress by E. Percy Moran; p. 20 Hulton Archive/Archive Photos/Getty Images.

Printed in the United States of America

CPSIA compliance information: Batch #CW13GS: For further information contact Gareth Stevens, New York, New York at 1-800-542-2595.

CONTENTS

Words in the glossary appear in **bold** type the first time they are used in the text.

WAR IN THE COLONIES

As the 1760s began, American **colonists** had become angry that the British king wasn't listening to their concerns. Though the colonists were British citizens, the British government had been increasing its control over the colonies without their consent. In 1775, the colonists began to fight for independence.

However, more than 2 million colonists lived in America by the mid-1770s—and not all of them wanted a **revolution**. Nonetheless, from children to government officials, the war affected lives throughout the colonies.

Did You Know?

Those who supported the revolution called themselves **patriots**. The British saw these colonists as **rebels** starting a **civil war**.

The first shots of the American Revolution occurred at the Battles of Lexington and Concord in Massachusetts.

MANY KINDS OF PATRIOTS

Who were the patriots of the American Revolution? Paul Revere raced through the night to tell revolutionary leaders that the British were coming. **Continental army** soldiers risked their lives on the battlefield. Others, such as Thomas Jefferson and Benjamin Franklin, worked on the plan for an independent government.

Some patriots' efforts aren't as well known. Even before the colonies declared independence, American spies put their lives in danger. During the war, men—and sometimes women—went behind British lines to find out their plans. They planted false reports, too!

Did You Know?

While the patriots' call for revolution was loud enough to spark a war, they weren't in the majority. Many colonists didn't know which side to support and tried to stay out of the war altogether.

Paul Revere was just one brave patriot who put his life in danger for the war effort.

LIVING AS A LOYALIST

Colonists who wanted to stay part of the British kingdom were called Loyalists or Tories. Historians say this group made up about 20 percent of the colonial population!

Some Loyalists joined the British forces to fight the patriots. If they were captured, these men were considered **traitors** by the patriots. Other Loyalists who voiced their support for the British were publicly covered in tar and feathers! Stories of this kind of treatment caused many Loyalists to **flee** to Canada or back to Great Britain.

Did You Know?

The patriots so disliked Loyalists that they passed laws against Loyalists throughout the colonies. Loyalists were forced to pay heavy taxes, give up their land, and leave public office.

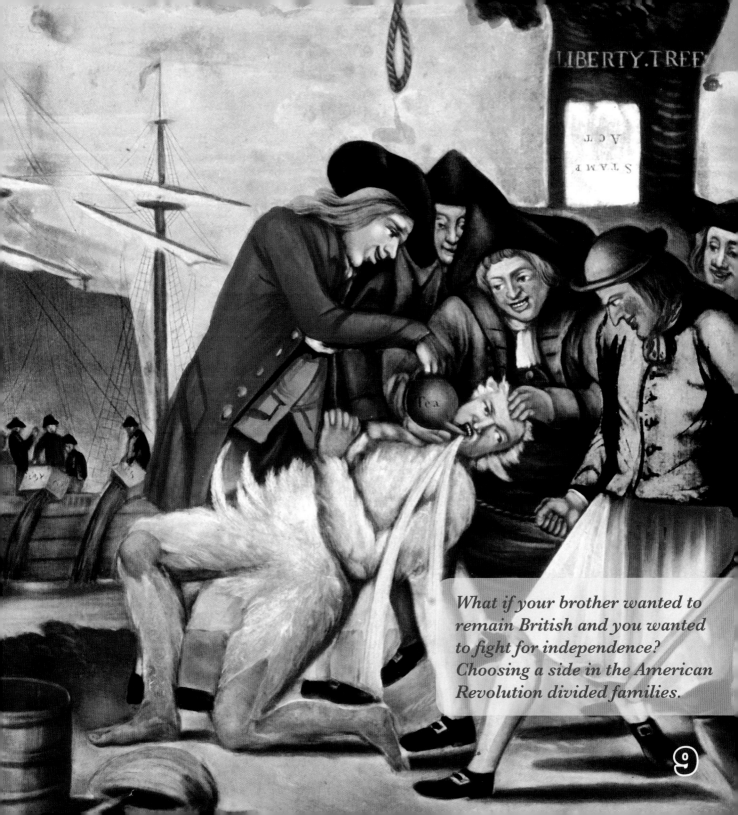

What if your brother wanted to remain British and you wanted to fight for independence? Choosing a side in the American Revolution divided families.

9

MILITIAMEN

Colonial men between the ages of 16 and 60 had to serve in their colony's militia. These small fighting forces tried to **defend** the colony's borders. However, the British army easily overcame the poorly trained militias.

Militiamen also supported the Continental army when the fighting came to their colony. However, the extra men that militias provided weren't always helpful to the patriot cause. The militias were commonly unorganized and undependable. In farming communities, militiamen would leave the battlefield when it was time to **harvest** their crops!

Did You Know?

George Washington didn't respect militiamen. He wrote that "to place any dependence upon militia is assuredly resting upon a broken staff."

Instead of joining the Continental army, most men chose to be part of a militia since they commonly fought near their homes and were able to choose their own leaders.

11

SOLDIERS WANTED

The Continental soldiers, led by George Washington, had little food, poor shelter, and a limited amount of clothing. There weren't even enough guns for men in battle! But the biggest supply problem for the Continental army was men.

Few wanted to join. Even when soldiers were paid or forced to sign up, the army was never as large as Washington wanted. The men who willingly signed up often didn't start out as good soldiers. They joined because they had few skills to bring them better opportunities.

Did You Know?

While many patriot soldiers didn't have shoes, they often had uniform coats or shirts of dark blue or brown. Through the thick smoke of battle, a man's coat was often all soldiers could use to tell who the enemy was.

Many soldiers had never been outside their home colony before the war. Some were meeting people from other colonies for the first time.

AT HOME DURING THE WAR

Bloody battles happened throughout the colonies during the American Revolution—sometimes right on a farmer's land or in a town square! Both armies took food and supplies from homes near their camps whether their owners were there or not. The British were known to set fire to the houses of patriot supporters, too.

When battles weren't nearby, colonists did the best they could to continue with everyday life. Shops still sold goods, families worked their farmland, and children went to school.

Did You Know?

Men who lost their jobs because of the British blockade sometimes found work with the Continental army—but not as soldiers. Support jobs, such as driving supply wagons, drew many men to the battlefront.

Many colonial families lost sons, brothers, and fathers to the war cause.

A WOMAN'S PLACE

In colonial society, women weren't equal to men. Men owned the family land and were the head of their household. Women cooked, cleaned, and cared for the children. But when the men left to fight during the American Revolution, women took charge at home.

In addition to keeping house, women throughout the colonies ran their husband's businesses and worked in the fields. Many women also had to stand up to forceful soldiers from both armies and guard their land.

Did You Know?

Following the war, women gained some equality in their families. In a letter, Abigail Adams famously asked her husband, future president John Adams, to "remember the ladies" when writing the plan for a new government.

While men fought on the battlefield, women fought to hold their family together and keep their home safe.

CAMP FOLLOWERS

Though many women stayed home during the war, others traveled with both the British and patriot forces. Many of these women, called camp followers, were soldiers' wives. They washed clothing, cooked, and helped care for the sick and wounded.

Some camp followers learned to fire cannons—just in case they were ever needed. One of these women, Margaret Corbin, put her knowledge to use in 1776 when her husband was killed while operating a cannon. This brave task earned her the nickname "Captain Molly."

Did You Know?

Camp followers with young children commonly brought them to travel with the soldiers. If the British captured a **regiment**, the camp followers were captured, too!

This illustration shows a woman nicknamed "Molly Pitcher" helping soldiers on the battlefield.

19

FREEMEN?

Some slaves earned their freedom by joining the British army or serving in their master's place in the Continental army. However, of the more than 400,000 slaves living in the colonies by the 1770s, most didn't fight in the war or gain independence after it ended.

About 5,000 slaves and free black men fought for the patriots. Many of them came from the North. Southern states didn't want many slaves fighting in the army. They feared slave rebellions if too many were armed.

The states' division on slavery was a big part of life during and after the American Revolution.

The American Revolution affected life in the colonies.

Women headed businesses and farms. Some were camp followers.

Men fought with militias and the Continental army.

Slaves were freed when they fought with the British.

Loyalists fled to Canada and Great Britain.

Patriot leaders wrote a new plan for government.

blockade: the blocking of harbors to keep people and supplies from coming and going

civil war: a war between two groups within a country

colonist: someone who lives in a colony

Continental army: the army of American colonists during the American Revolution, led by General George Washington

defend: to keep something safe

flee: to run away

harvest: to bring in a crop

patriot: a person who loves their country

rebel: someone who opposes a government. Also, openly opposing a government.

regiment: a military unit made up of smaller military units

revolution: a movement to overthrow an established government

traitor: a person who is not faithful to another person or group

FOR MORE INFORMATION

Books

Catel, Patrick. *The Home Front of the Revolutionary War.* Chicago, IL: Heinemann Library, 2011.

Forest, Christopher. *The Rebellious Colonists and the Causes of the American Revolution.* North Mankato, MN: Capstone Press, 2013.

McNeese, Tim. *Revolutionary America, 1764–1789.* New York, NY: Chelsea House, 2010.

Websites

American Revolution
www.history.com/topics/american-revolution
Read and watch videos about the events of the American Revolution.

American Revolution Timeline
timeline.americanrevolutioncenter.org
Read more about the history of the American Revolution and see items from that time period in this interactive timeline.

Index